2/15

ANIMALS OF MASS DESTRUCTION

CARPENTER ANTS

 Gareth Stevens
PUBLISHING

By Katherine Ponka

Please visit our website, www.garethstevens.com. For a free color catalog of all our high-quality books, call toll free 1-800-542-2595 or fax 1-877-542-2596.

Library of Congress Cataloging-in-Publication Data

Ponka, Katherine.
Carpenter ants / by Katherine Ponka.
 p. cm. — (Animals of mass destruction)
Includes index.
ISBN 978-1-4824-1025-9 (pbk.)
ISBN 978-1-4824-1026-6 (6-pack)
ISBN 978-1-4824-1024-2 (library binding)
1. Insect pests — Juvenile literature. 2. Ants — Juvenile literature. 3. Carpenter ants. I. Title.
QL568.F7 P66 2014
595.79—d23

First Edition

Published in 2015 by
Gareth Stevens Publishing
111 East 14th Street, Suite 349
New York, NY 10003

Copyright © 2015 Gareth Stevens Publishing

Designer: Andrea Davison-Bartolotta
Editor: Therese Shea

Photo credits: Cover, p. 1 (main), 28 iStock/Thinkstock; cover, pp. 1 (inset), 6, 14 Henrik Larsson/Shutterstock.com; series art (all textured backgrounds, yellow striped line) Elisanth/Shutterstock.com; series art (caption boxes) Fatseyeva/Shutterstock.com; series art (green boxes) Tracie Andrews/Shutterstock.com; p. 4 Bondarenko/Shutterstock.com; p. 5 Joel Sartore/National Geographic/Getty Images; p. 7 BW Folsom/Shutterstock.com; pp. 8, 10, 13, 14, 18, 22, 24 (ant silhouette) Aleks Melnik/Shutterstock.com; p. 8 © iStockphoto.com/PaulTessier; p. 9 Scott Camazine/Photo Researchers/Getty Images; pp. 11, 25 Kenneth H. Thomas/Photo Researchers/Getty Images; p. 12 Tomatito/Shutterstock.com; p. 13 David Wrobel/Visuals Unlimited/Getty Images; p. 15 Kurt M/Shutterstock.com; p. 16 Paul Beard/Photodisc/Getty Images; p. 17 Gawrave Sinha/Vetta/Getty Images; p. 18 Hamik/Shutterstock.com; p. 19 Bruce MacQueen/Shutterstock.com; p. 20 Frank Zullo/Photo Researchers/Getty Images; p. 21 Andrey Pavlov/Shutterstock.com; p. 23 (inset) pabkov/Thinkstock; p. 23 (main) Smith Chetanachan/Thinkstock; p. 24 MP cz/Shutterstock.com; p. 27 Bykofoto/Shutterstock.com; p. 29 Rustam Burganov/Shutterstock.com.

Printed in the United States of America

CPSIA compliance information: Batch #CS15GS: For further information contact Gareth Stevens, Now York, New York at 1-800-542-2595.

CONTENTS

Words in the glossary appear in **bold** type the first time they are used in the text.

ANTS EVERYWHERE!

When you sit in the grass, you don't have to wait very long before an ant goes by. That's because ants are some of the most numerous creatures on Earth. There are more than 1,000 kinds of carpenter ants alone.

Carpenter ants get their name because they make their homes out of wood, just like a carpenter might. However, carpenter ants actually live *in* the wood and chew through it. When they choose wooden buildings for their nests, they can be very **destructive**!

Carpenter ants tunnel through wood by chewing it.
They don't eat the wood, though.

5

INSIDE AND OUT

Outside, carpenter ants aid nature by making their homes in dead or rotting trees. This helps the trees break down and mix with soil, so new trees can grow. However, chewing tunnels in wood buildings weakens the buildings. If not found early, carpenter ants can be very harmful to wood structures.

Carpenter ants keep their nests tidy and clean. They push out sawdust, dirt, and even dead bug parts! Tiny piles of this matter, called frass, are one way to spot ant activity both inside and outside.

carpenter ant

Carpenter ants leave piles of sawdust behind as they work. You might even hear them chewing inside walls!

SOCIAL ANIMALS

One reason carpenter ants are so destructive is that they don't act alone. They live in large colonies.

In late spring or early summer, male winged carpenter ants, called swarmers, **mate** in midair with winged female carpenter ants. The males die after mating. The females lose their wings and become queen ants.

A colony starts when a queen ant is ready to lay her eggs. Her colony is small at first, but can contain up to 3,000 ants within 3 years.

Chew On This!

Queen carpenter ants can live more than 20 years!

swarmer

A queen carpenter ant tends her young.

TOUGH MOTHER

Before the queen carpenter ant lays her eggs, she finds soft, rotting wood to make her nest. In houses, she targets wooden areas around chimneys, window frames, porches, and roofs. These are places that are often cracked or **moist** from leaks.

The queen then seals herself into the space and lays 15 to 20 eggs. She feeds on stored body fat and on her wing **muscles**. After the eggs hatch, the queen carpenter ant feeds her young with liquids from her body.

Chew On This!

The Hopi Indians tell an ancient story in which the first people were cared for by ant people deep within the earth.

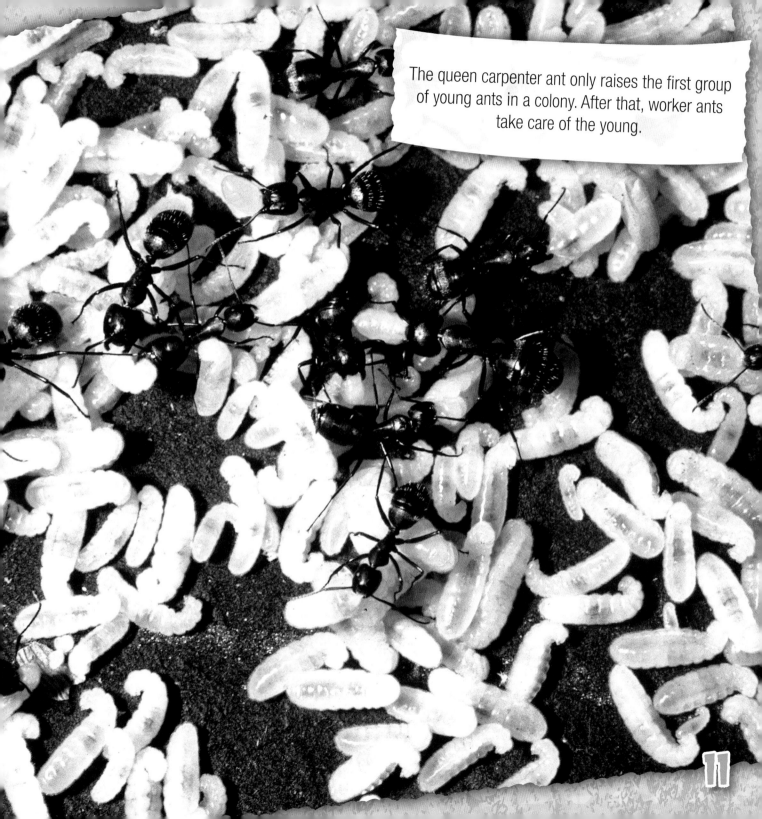

The queen carpenter ant only raises the first group of young ants in a colony. After that, worker ants take care of the young.

LIFE CYCLE OF A CARPENTER ANT

A carpenter ant begins life as an oval-shaped egg, sometimes less than 0.04 inch (1 mm) long. After it hatches, it enters the **larva** stage. It looks like a worm and has no eyes. The larva sheds its skin many times as it grows.

In the **pupa** stage, the ant builds a cocoon and attaches itself to the wall of the nest. In its cocoon, its body begins to change to look like an adult ant. Finally, the adult ant comes out of the cocoon.

stages of an ant's life

It takes 6 to 12 weeks for a carpenter ant to grow from an egg to an adult.

adult

pupa

larva

eggs

Chew On This!

When nests are bothered, ants may bite and spray a **chemical** called formic acid that can be very painful!

TIRELESS WORKERS

Most carpenter ants are wingless females called worker ants. A colony needs lots of workers. These females can't lay eggs, but they do many other jobs. They tend to the queen and the young, clean the nest, gather food, and defend the colony from predators.

After about 2 years in the nest, the queen begins to produce winged males and winged females. As adults, these carpenter ants mate and leave the nest to begin new colonies.

Chew On This!

Each colony of ants has its own smell!

worker ant

Carpenter ant colonies can be many sizes, but each colony has one queen and many worker ants.

ANT SENSES

Carpenter ants are among the largest ants in North America. They have compound eyes, which contain hundreds of lenses. The queen and male ants also have three single eyes, called ocelli (oh-SEH-ly), on top of their head to sense light.

Carpenter ants give and receive messages by touching each other's **antennae**. They tell each other where food and danger are. They also use their antennae to smell chemicals called pheromones (FEHR-uh-mohnz). Pheromones are left behind as a trail for other ants. That makes it easy for them to find food!

You can see this ant's compound eyes as it raises its legs in an attack.

MIDNIGHT SNACKS

Carpenter ants are omnivores, which means they eat both plants and animals. They feed on bugs and worms, dead or alive. They also like sugar. One of their favorite sugar sources is the liquid produced by **aphids** called honeydew.

When worker ants can't find enough food outside, they make their way into homes. They like meats and sweets they find there. That's why they're often found in kitchens. Carpenter ants gather food at night, returning to the nest by the next morning.

aphids

Chew On This!

Carpenter ants like honeydew so much that they guard aphids from danger.

Aphids suck liquids from plants to make honeydew. The ant will move them once the plant runs out of liquid.

TWO TUMMIES!

A carpenter ant's **abdomen** is the largest part of its body. It holds two stomachs! Each stomach has a separate job. One holds food that will be shared with the ant's colony. The other stomach holds food for the ant itself.

Adult carpenter ants don't eat solid food. They suck juices out of solid foods and store them in their bodies. However, ant larvae do eat solid food, so worker ants bring it back to the nest for them.

Ants feed each other mouth to mouth. They look like they're kissing!

abdomen

CARPENTER ANTS OR TERMITES?

Carpenter ants are often confused with termites. However, they look different. A termite's body is made up of two main parts, while a carpenter ant's body has three main parts. A termite's antennae are straight, while a carpenter ant's antennae are bent.

Carpenter ants and termites also act differently. Carpenter ants chew through wood, but termites actually eat wood. In fact, termites are even more destructive than carpenter ants!

Chew On This!

When termites sense danger, they bang their heads against walls to warn other termites!

Worker termites, like these, are almost white.

carpenter ant

termites

23

ANT TRACKER

If you see large black ants crawling around in your kitchen, it could mean a carpenter ant nest is in your home. Check any areas on the inside and outside of the house where moisture may have gotten into the wood. Remember, these are favorite spots for carpenter ants to build their nests.

You may not find a nest. Sometimes, carpenter ants nest outdoors but come in looking for food for themselves and for the ants back at the colony.

Chew On This!

Ants can carry 10 to 15 times their body weight!

When wooden buildings aren't cared for, carpenter ants can take over!

KEEP OUT!

As cute as you might think carpenter ants are, you don't want them living in your home. Remember, they harm the wood that makes up your house.

To get rid of ants, some home owners coat sugar with chemicals. The ants take this sugar back to the nest, and it poisons the whole colony.

There are less harmful ways to keep ants out of your home, too. Ants don't like cucumber peels, so people put them in certain places to stop ants from coming in. Ants also hate cinnamon and pepper!

Ants love to eat food left on a kitchen counter. They also eat garbage and pet food!

HELPFUL AND HARMFUL

Carpenter ants play an important part in nature by making their homes in rotting trees and helping them break down. They also keep the populations of bugs down by eating them.

However, carpenter ants become destructive when they tunnel into buildings and weaken them. They're also pests when they get into our homes and eat our food. Make sure you clean up after preparing food. If you don't, carpenter ants might think you're leaving a snack for them!

Carpenter ants are breaking down this old tree. Notice the piles of frass left behind.

29

GLOSSARY

abdomen: the part of an insect's body that contains the stomach

antenna: a feeler on the head of some animals. The plural of "antenna" is "antennae."

aphid: a sap-sucking, soft-bodied bug about the size of a pinhead

chemical: matter that can be mixed with other matter to cause changes

destructive: causing a lot of damage

larva: a bug in an early life stage that has a wormlike form. The plural form is "larvae."

mate: to come together to make babies

moist: a bit wet or damp

muscle: one of the parts of the body that allow movement

pupa: a bug that is changing from a larva to an adult, usually inside a case or cocoon. The plural form is "pupae."

FOR MORE INFORMATION

Books

Birch, Robin. *Ants Up Close*. Chicago, IL: Raintree Press, 2005.

Murray, Julie. *Ants*. ABDO Publishing, 2010.

Peterson, Megan Cooley. *Look Inside an Ant Nest*. Mankato, MN: Capstone Press, 2012.

Websites

Ants in General
www.antweb.org
Learn about carpenter ants as well as many different kinds of ants.

Carpenter Ants
www1.extension.umn.edu/garden/insects/find/carpenter-ants/
Read more about carpenter ants and their lives.

INDEX